GETTING TO KNOW THE WORLD'S GREATEST INVENTORS & SCIENTISTS

THE
WRIGHT
BROTHERS

Inventors Whose Ideas Really Took Flight

WRITTEN AND ILLUSTRATED BY MIKE VENEZIA

CHILDREN'S PRESS®
AN IMPRINT OF SCHOLASTIC INC.
NEW YORK   TORONTO   LONDON   AUCKLAND   SYDNEY
MEXICO CITY   NEW DELHI   HONG KONG
DANBURY, CONNECTICUT

Content Consultant: Darrell Collins, Chief Historian and Interpreter, Wright Brothers
National Memorial, Kill Devil Hills, North Carolina

Reading Consultant: Nanci R. Vargus, Ed.D., Assistant Professor, School of Education,
University of Indianapolis

Photographs © 2010: akg-Images, London: 27; Brown Brothers: 5 bottom; Corbis Images: 13 (Bettmann), 15 top (Smithsonian Institution); Dayton Metro Library/Wright Brothers Collection: 10 bottom; Everett Collection, Inc./AISA: 4 left; Fernando Gomes Semedo, www.nando.ca: 22; Getty Images: 17 (Hulton Archive), 21 (Library of Congress), 23 (London Stereoscopic Company), 4 right, 6, 7 (Time Life Pictures/Mansell), 26 (Topical Press Agency); Mary Evans Picture Library: 5 top; North Wind Picture Archives: 28; Photo Researchers, NY/US Air Force: 29; Smithsonian Institution, Washington, DC/National Air and Space Museum: 15 bottom; The Granger Collection, New York: 10 top, 14, 16; The Image Works: 25 (akg-images), 20 (Science Museum/SSPL), 31 (SSPL), 3 (Topham).

Colorist for illustrations: Andrew Day

Library of Congress Cataloging-in-Publication Data

Venezia, Mike.
  The Wright brothers : inventors whose ideas really took flight /
written and illustrated by Mike Venezia.
     p. cm. — (Getting to know the world's greatest inventors and
scientists)
  Includes index.
  ISBN-13: 978-0-531-23732-8 (lib. bdg.)   978-0-531-22353-6 (pbk.)
  ISBN-10: 0-531-23732-X (lib. bdg.)   0-531-22353-1 (pbk.)
  1. Wright, Wilbur, 1867–1912—Juvenile literature. 2. Wright,
Orville, 1871–1948—Juvenile literature. 3. Aeronautics—United
States—Biography—Juvenile literature. 4. Aeronautics—United
States—History—Juvenile literature. I. Title. II. Series.

TL540.W7V458 2010
629.130092'273—dc22
[B]
                              2009030222

Orville (left) and
Wilbur Wright
in 1910

Wilbur and Orville Wright are famous for inventing and flying the world's first engine-powered aircraft. After five years of hard work, the Wright brothers solved the mystery of flight. They changed our lives and the world of transportation forever.

This is an illustration of a flying machine imagined by Italian artist Leonardo da Vinci in 1487. Leonardo drew plans for a number of flying machines, but none were actually created.

In 1785, Jean-Pierre Blanchard and John Jeffries became the first people to cross the English Channel in a hydrogen-filled balloon.

For thousands of years, people had been trying to find a way to fly. Inventors and scientists dreamed about building a flying machine.

In the 1800s, many people attempted to build machines that would allow them to fly like birds. None of these flying machines were successful, however.

Eventually, some daring inventors came up with ways to sail through the air on **gliders** or rise into the sky with hot air balloons. But no one ever came close to figuring out how to power a heavier-than-air flying machine and control it with a pilot aboard.

No one, that is, until the Wright brothers
made their first flight on a chilly, deserted
beach in Kitty Hawk, North Carolina.
On December 17, 1903, Orville lifted off
the ground for twelve seconds. He flew a
distance of 120 feet and landed safely.

Orville is at the controls and Wilbur is at right in this photograph of the world's first successful engine-powered airplane flight, in 1903. The Wrights called their machine a "Flyer." The term *airplane* didn't come into use until 1907.

Then Wilbur gave it a try. The brothers spent the rest of the morning taking turns. By noon, Wilbur kept their flying machine in the air for 59 seconds and flew a distance of 852 feet. No one in the history of the world had ever flown in the air that long before!

Wilbur Wright was born in 1867 near Millville, Indiana. Four years later, in 1871, Orville was born. By this time their family had moved to Dayton, Ohio. The Wright brothers spent most of their lives living and working in Dayton. Wil and Orv had two older brothers and a younger sister. Their father was a minister and church leader.

Mr. Wright was often away on church business. Mrs. Wright did a great job running the household on her own. She had a special talent for making and fixing things. She knew how to use tools and was always building shelves, tables, and chairs. She made clothes as well as toys for her kids. Wil and Orv definitely took after their mom when it came to inventing and building things.

Wilbur Wright as a child

Mr. Wright helped influence his sons in other ways. He often brought unusual and fun toys home with him when he returned from long business trips. One toy in particular excited Wil and Orv. It was a rubber-band-powered flying gadget that looked kind of like a helicopter. The brothers couldn't believe it. They had never seen a toy that could fly!

Orville Wright at age four

Wil and Orv called their new toy the "bat" because it reminded them of a bat flying around the house. They played with it for hours until it finally fell apart. Then they tried to build their own bat. Even though their toy bat didn't work very well, the experience stirred up the boys' imagination.

While growing up, the Wright brothers enjoyed making their own kites and other toys. They were always taking things apart—like old sewing machines—to see if they could put them back together correctly. The brothers wanted to know how everything worked.

In 1889, Wil and Orv went into the printing business together and published a local paper called the *West Side News*. After a few years, though, the Wright brothers began to lose interest in the printing business. They decided to try something completely new and different. In the 1890s, bicycling had become a popular craze in the United States. Wil and Orv loved riding and repairing their own bikes. They thought opening a cycle shop might be the perfect business for them.

In the 1890s, when the new sport of bicycling became popular (above), Orville and Wilbur opened a bicycle shop.

Wilbur and Orville started the Wright Cycle Company in 1892. At first, they sold popular brands of bicycles and repaired broken bikes. But before long, the brothers started designing and building their own bicycles.

Wilbur Wright works in the bicycle shop in 1897.

This is one of only five original Wright brothers
bicycles that still exist today.

By 1898, Wil and Orv had become well known for their excellent mechanical skills. They sold lots of bicycles and became quite successful.

The Wright brothers were inspired by German inventor Otto Lilienthal (right), who built and flew early gliders.

The Wright brothers had always been interested in anything mechanical. They were especially fascinated by anything having to do with flight. Wil and Orv couldn't wait to read the latest magazine articles about what was going on in **aviation** at the time. One of their heroes was a German inventor named Otto Lilienthal. Otto had been successful in building and flying gliders. But one day, the brothers were shocked to learn that Lilienthal had been killed when his glider suddenly crashed into the ground.

Both Wil and Orv wondered what could have gone wrong. What had caused Lilienthal to lose control of the glider? This tragic event really sparked the brothers' desire to learn more about flight. Wilbur began to collect as much information as he could from the local library. He later wrote to the Smithsonian Institution, requesting other reading materials on the subject of human flight.

Otto Lilienthal gets ready to take off in one of his gliders in 1893.

A well-known flight **enthusiast** named Octave Chanute had spent years researching the history of flying and was willing to share his findings with the Wright brothers. The brothers did their own research, too, by closely observing birds in flight.

Wil and Orv discovered that birds tilted their wings to lean into turns and to move up and down in the air. The Wright brothers knew that gliders, like Lilienthal's, sailed through the air on wings that were rigid. They thought that if they could make a glider wing that was flexible, like a bird's wing, they could build a successful flying machine. The only problem was that they had no idea how to do it.

Then, one day, Wilbur made an amazing discovery. While in the cycle shop, he absentmindedly twisted a long, narrow, cardboard inner tube box. He noticed that when he tilted one end of the box up, the other end tilted down. This was similar to the way birds worked their wings. The Wright brothers called Wilbur's discovery **wing warping**.

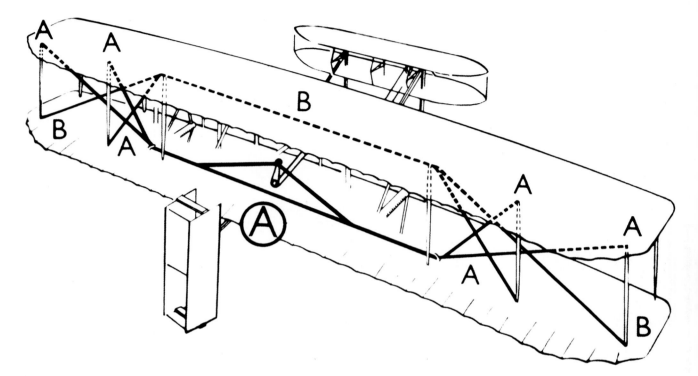

This diagram shows the cable system used to produce wing warping on a Wright brothers aircraft. The cables allowed one wing tip to be raised while the other was lowered.

In 1899, to see if wing warping worked, the brothers built a five-foot kite based on Wilbur's idea. With wing warping, you could change the way air flowed over and around a wing and turn a flying machine to the right or left.

Wilbur tested the kite in a field outside of Dayton. He controlled the kite from the ground with strings attached to the wings. Wil was able to move the kite up and down and turn it to the right and left. The brothers learned that wing warping was the key to solving the problem of control. This was a major step forward in the history of aviation.

In 1900, the Wrights tested a glider that worked the same way as their 1899 kite.

Wil and Orv were very excited. With the success of the 1899 kite, they were now ready to build a glider big enough to carry a man onboard to control wing warping. They got to work right away. The bicycle shop was the perfect place to build their glider. It had all the tools and machinery the brothers needed.

The interior of Orville and Wilbur's bike shop has been re-created at Greenfield Village in Dearborn, Michigan.

As these acrobats show, riding a bicycle requires balance and control. The Wrights' understanding of this was very helpful to them when they were designing their early Flyers.

Working with bicycles gave the Wright brothers an advantage over other flying pioneers. Wil and Orv really understood the importance of balance and control in riding a bicycle safely. They applied this knowledge to building and piloting their flying machine.

While they were building their glider, Wil checked around to find a good place to test it. He decided that Kitty Hawk, a seaside town in North Carolina, would be just right. It had steady winds, plenty of open space, and nice, soft sand to land on. In 1900, Wil and Orv tested their first glider. They shipped it to Kitty Hawk in pieces by train, and then by boat.

The brothers set up a tent shelter and assembled the glider on the beach. At first, they flew it unmanned, as they had done with their 1899 kite. Later, Orville and a helpful Kitty Hawk resident launched the glider with Wil aboard. Even though Wil's flight ended quickly when he began to lose control, the brothers were happy with the result. Wil and Orv headed back to Dayton, anxious to build an improved glider.

Orville (far left) and Wilbur (piloting glider) test a glider in 1902.

The Wright brothers returned to Kitty Hawk two more times to test different gliders and improve their flying skills. Wil and Orv worked hard to adjust the wing shapes to help lift the glider more successfully. They found new ways to **stabilize** and control the glider by adding a moveable tail **rudder**. Finally, the brothers felt ready to add an engine and **propellers** to power their Flyer through the air.

The Wright brothers continued to test gliders even after their famous engine-powered 1903 flight. This is a photo of Orville taking a bad landing in a 1911 glider.

Orville and Wilbur with one of their Flyers in 1904

Back in Dayton, the brothers constructed their largest Flyer yet. It had a forty-foot **wingspan** and included propellers and a gasoline engine. In 1903, Wil and Orv headed back to Kitty Hawk and made history. They were the first to fly a heavier-than-air engine-powered aircraft.

But the brothers still had a lot of work to do. Wilbur and Orville spent the next few years building more powerful Flyers and perfecting their flying skills.

Wilbur Wright swoops over a hay field in France in 1908.

By 1908, Orville had made flights that lasted over an hour. Wilbur amazed thousands of people in France by doing figure eights over the crowd. The Wright brothers did public demonstrations to get attention. They hoped to find a customer who would be willing to buy their flying machines.

In 1909, Orville impressed the U.S. Army by flying a two-seater plane with a passenger onboard. The Army Signal Corps agreed to purchase the Wright Flyer for $30,000. Soon, the Wright brothers received more orders. Later that year, they set up the Wright Company to build and sell airplanes. They also opened a school to train pilots. Over the next few years, the brothers built bigger airplanes that could fly farther and faster and could carry more weight.

This 1914 photograph shows a model F, one of the Wrights' later planes. The model F was the first Wright aircraft to have a **fuselage,** a partially enclosed area for the pilot.

Soon, other airplane manufacturing companies began popping up in the United States and Europe. The age of flying had begun. In less than seventy years, humans went from flying an engine-powered aircraft a few hundred feet to launching the Saturn V rocket. In 1969, only 66 years after the Wright brothers' first flight at Kitty Hawk, a Saturn V rocket carried three American astronauts 240,000 miles to the moon. This amazing leap in flight technology all started with two very imaginative, daring, and inventive brothers.

Sadly, in 1912, just when The Wright Company was becoming really successful, Wilbur became ill with **typhoid fever.** He died a short time later, at the age of 45. After that, Orville pretty much lost interest in the flying business. He sold the company and lived a quiet life. Orville was often called on to offer advice and join **aeronautic** committees. He passed away peacefully in 1948 at his home in Dayton, Ohio.

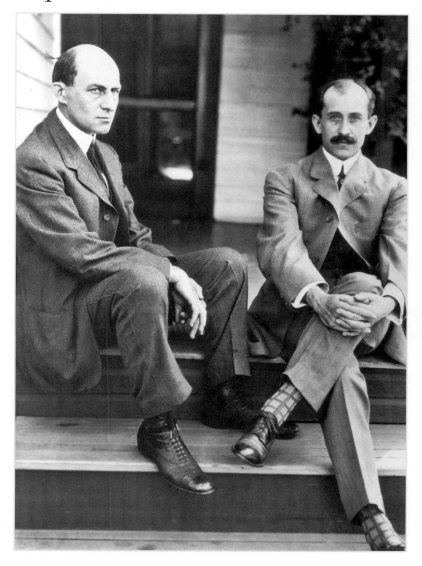

Wilbur (left) and Orville in 1909

Glossary

aeronautic (air-uh-NAW-tik) Relating to the science or practice of travel through the air

aviation (ay-vee-AY-shuhn) The science of building and flying aircraft

enthusiast (en-THOO-zee-ist) Someone who is very interested in a particular hobby or activity

fuselage (FYOO-suh-lahzh) The enclosed or partially enclosed part of an aircraft where the passengers, crew, and cargo are carried

glider (GLIDE-ur) A very light aircraft that has no engine and that flies by floating and rising on air currents

propeller (pruh-PEL-ur) A set of rotating blades that provide force to move a vehicle through air or water

rudder (RUHD-ur) A wood or metal plate attached to the back of an airplane or boat and used for steering

stabilize (STAY-buhl-ize) To make something hold steady

typhoid fever (TYE-foid FEE-vur) A serious infectious disease with symptoms of high fever and diarrhea

wingspan (WING-span) The distance between the outer tips of the wings of a bird or aircraft

wing warping (WING WORP-ing) A system for control of an aircraft in which, through a system of pulleys and cables, the aircraft's wings are twisted in opposite directions

Index

Army Signal Corps, 29
Chanute, Octave, 18
da Vinci, Leonardo, 4
Dayton, Ohio, 8, 15, 25, 27, 31
early flying machines, 4–5, 16–17
fuselage, 29
glider, 5, 16–17, 21, 22, 24–26
hot air balloons, 5
hydrogen air balloon, 4
Kitty Hawk, North Carolina, 6, 24, 25, 26, 27
Lilienthal, Otto, 16–17

Millville, Indiana, 8
propeller, 26
rudder, 26
Saturn V rocket, 30
typhoid fever, 31
wing warping, 19–21, 22
Wright, Orville and Wilbur
  as children, 8–12
  bicycle shop, 13–15, 19, 22
  deaths of, 31
  first engine-powered flight, 3, 6–7, 27, 30
  model F airplane, 29

public demonstrations, 28
pilot-training school, 29
printing business, 12–13
research of, 16–19, 23
testing of gliders, 22–26
testing of kite, 20–22
two-seater plane, 29